THE BREAK-UP
BOSS

The Break-Up Boss

HOW TO BREAKUP WITH TOXIC PEOPLE AND MINDSETS THAT KEEP YOU DOWN

Jeanine Elise Mack, MSL

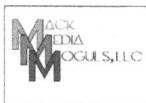

Mack Media Moguls, LLC

Copyright

ISBN-13: 978-1733490887

Dedication

I dedicate this book to every lonely heart, broken heart, fractured heart, happy heart, content heart and brave heart; that is attempting to trust again, love again, heal and restore again – I open my heart to you. You are my reason for writing this book. I know that your best days are in front of you....so keep loving, keep healing and most of all, keep believing in yourself!

With Love,
Jeanine

Special Thanks

I want to thank everyone who worked with me to make this book come to life. You all challenged me, inspired me, encouraged me and pushed my creativity as an author, writer and human being - into a place that has made me better. I'm forever grateful to you all!

Cover Photography: Jerrard Mack with Flashefx
Photography
Cover Design: Vandalay Parë
Book Editing: Monique Mensah with Make Your
Mark Publishing Solutions

Contents

Foreward: Dr. Linda M. Pittenger

The "Break Up Boss" authored by Jeanine E. Mack takes you on a passage of personal musings supported by creative pieces of poetry. The book provides much insight and offers the reader the opportunity to reflect on his or her own journey. Exercises in the book enable the reader to reflect on the content and then journal their thoughts.

I had the pleasure of being one of Jeanine's professors in the Masters of Leadership program at Embry Riddle Aeronautical University. I have many students in my classes each year, but there are always those few special students that are unforgettable. Jeanine is one of those students. Within the program, Jeanine was encouraged to reflect deeply on her "ideal self", to clearly see who she could be when she is at her best, living healthily, and happy. She also focused on discovering her "real self". The "real self" is who she is today, how she engages with others, and what are her strengths and weaknesses. After these reflections, Jeanine finalized a plan to address the gaps between her "real and ideal self" and build on her strengths.

This book represents a part of Jeanine's "ideal self". Her

passion for self-development and helping others is evidenced in the contents of this book. It is exciting to see that Jeanine is well on her way to becoming her "ideal self". "The Break Up Boss" will propel you to begin your journey to becoming your ideal self. Congratulations to you! Start reading…you deserve this!

Dr. Linda M. Pittenger
Associate Professor
Embry Riddle Aeronautical University

Introduction

Hello, friend! I'm so glad you have chosen to take your life and relationships to the next level. I'll be with you every step of the way as you elevate to a new level of freedom. The main purpose of this book is to be a source of healing and a guide of methods, solutions, and confidence builders. I'll show you how to recognize and respectfully end bad relationships, destructive life cycles, and defective thinking patterns. During and after every negative relationship breakup I've experienced, I promised myself I would share my experiences, so others would not have to suffer my same fate. This is me fulfilling that promise to myself and to you. My hope is that you will see your life in these pages and something you read will spark and energize you to make a change. Similar to how the caterpillar must go through a quiet and secluded cocoon stage to become a beautiful butterfly, we must take the necessary steps to break free of our old relationship habits to fully receive the love we so desperately desire and deserve.

I want the best for you, just as I do for those closest to me. You can certainly do this, and I'll be there with you every step of the way! From this day forward, don't ever think you are the only one who has experienced bad relationships. The good news is after you have taken the journey in this book, you will be able to recognize when someone is not right for you, and you'll have a plan for how to end that bad relationship in a positive manner. Yes, there are signs, red flags, or gut feelings—whatever you choose to call them—that are present from the onset of a relationship. The disaster comes when we make the choice to ignore those signs. But no more! By the time you have finished reading this book, you will have the confidence to say no, reclaim your peace of mind, and never go back to the vicious cycle of broken relationships.

To solve a problem, you have to get to the core of why the problem exists. Many times, we get into romantic relationships because society says we should be in love. Due to the high commercialization of engagement and wedding jewelry, dating websites and apps, reality TV matchmaking shows, and even reality TV wedding shows, we think something is wrong with us if we aren't experiencing those things in our lives. In turn, we seek out someone to fulfill that unnecessary void, usually Mr. or Ms. Wrong. If you've come across a Mr. or Ms. Wrong in your life, it's time to usher them to the exit! If you don't know how, The Break Up Boss is here to teach you the art of breaking up and breaking free. Don't spend another year, month, week, day, or minute trying to resuscitate a relationship that was dead from the start. Stop wasting your time, my friend! The only person you can change is you.

If you don't recognize your value, if you are having trouble loving yourself, or if you don't know how to break free from negativity, I have provided original poetry pieces and personal affirmation statements that were born out of my relationship struggles, heartbreaks, and eventually, my victories. You'll also be able to express your thoughts and write your own success story as we go through each chapter of this book. Your growth has to be measurable, and you will see your transformation from chapter to chapter and definitely by the completion of this book, which is not an ending, but the beginning of a brand new chapter of your life.

Are you ready? Just the fact that you are reading this book tells me you are, so let's begin your beautiful transformation from caterpillar to butterfly and from breakup recipient to Break Up Boss. Let's go!

How Did I Get Into This Mess?

Poem: "Self Inflicted"

"Self Inflicted"

Self-inflicted and so vindictive
about my wounded heart that you conflicted.
I never pushed a broom so hard to pick up the pieces of
my broken heart.
Broken and bruised with the memories of you...
I've lost this love game, and now I'm ashamed!
I tried not to be the fool, the source of ridicule,
But I reverse it back to me, and I've lost my cool!
So the pain I feel is self-inflicted;
I committed this love crime, and now I'm convicted.

You showed me your hate, but I loved you anyway.
You showed me disrespect, but I respected you
every day.
You showed me only lust, but I gave you intimacy.
You showed me no time, but I was never too busy.
I was your secret cheat, but you were my First Love.
The pedestal I had you on is so high above
The reality of what you and I could never be!

I knew you weren't right for me, not good for me,
so bad for me, so why didn't I leave?
Because, obviously, I enjoy the pleasure of pain,
which sounds so insane, but who's to blame?
Self-inflicted wounds of the heart, emotional turmoil
in my spirit; I know you don't want to hear it!
But this is my song, and I'll sing it loud
To warn the foolish lovers in this crowd!
After all the smoke clears from my mental wasteland,
Sadly, but surely, I'll visit this dark place again!
Longing, rescinded, captured, abandoned, given,
demanded, hoped for, disappointed, but the truth of
my pain…was self-inflicted!

—Jeanine Mack, 8/1/2010

1

Chapter 1: How Did I Get into This Mess?

Chapter 1: How Did I Get into This Mess?

"How did I get into this mess?" is the number one rhetorical question I hear from many unhappy people seeking an answer about their discontent in their current relationships. Although, on the surface, this seems to be a complex and unanswerable question, the reality is you don't suddenly appear in a bad relationship; you've taken several steps to get there. Most of those steps were subconscious because we tend to put our common sense on autopilot when we see or meet someone who appeals to our eyes and ignites the flames of lust and passion within us. Truth be told, deep down inside, there is a little voice that says a clear and unwavering, No, do not proceed! Now, if we choose to acknowledge and obey that voice, our lives will continue on the path to success. However, if we choose to ignore and disobey that voice, we ultimately alter the course of our lives into a direction that was never meant for us. Let's examine a few relationship mistakes that lead us down a slippery slope toward unhappy relationships.

The Why Behind the What

Just when you think you're the only person experiencing the "bad relationship blues," you are not! Actually, there are some relationship mistakes that are more common than most of us would care to admit. The main headliners are:

- Eye Candy Appeal
- Lonely Hearts Club
- Approval Ratings
- Judgement Day
- Religious Rights
- Financial Fantasy

Eye Candy Appeal

"Everything that glitters ain't gold!" my mother would say to my siblings and me. I heard this cliché on numerous occasions throughout my childhood, and I finally understood it in my adulthood—particularly in the area of romantic relationships. The Eye Candy Appeal is the phenomenon of selecting a partner based solely on how that person looks and what makes them attractive to us. This can include their physical features, their clothing, material possessions, job, home, the way they walk, the sound of their voice and their charming words, or whatever else makes that person appealing to our eyes. Fool's gold often glitters like real gold, and the same can be said about the visual appeal or attractiveness of a person, even though this does not determine how good they are for us.

All of these visual luxuries have absolutely nothing to do with the person's inward qualities, yet we often choose a partner and/or spouse based solely on these appealing attributes. It sounds very shallow when reading this on the page, and you may be thinking to yourself, I'm not a shallow person, but I like what I like! Now, I'm not downplaying the importance of being physically attracted to someone you are interested in; however, when that becomes the foremost quality used to choose a partner, you are headed for disaster. Our eyes can really deceive us and make us believe that if someone looks good then they are good and, therefore, are good for us. We must be aware of this troubling trend of superficial beauty and skin-deep goodness. How can anyone be a good partner to you if you don't know who that person is once their makeup comes off, their hair weave comes out, the nice car is parked, their jewelry is removed, and all material possessions are no longer around?

Even though I don't like this trend in dating, I'm not surprised by it. We currently live in a society where beauty sells everything, from hamburgers to cars, and commercials and movies are presented in HD, 3D, and dynamic imaging. The images of Hollywood and internet stars alike lead us to believe that beauty and perfection equal love and likability. Conversely, as the old adage goes, "Beauty fades." Therefore, outward beauty should not be the sole premise for partner selection. I urge you to dig deeper than the surface to discover the core of your eye candy's being; you may just find what you always knew would be there: nothing! No depth of character, no constructive conversation, no care, and no love—all a big waste of time and effort for you.

I, too, have been guilty of using the Eye Candy Appeal to select a partner. Unfortunately, this happened more than once because, apparently, I didn't learn my lesson the first ten times, but I'll give this particular example. In my hometown, I would always see the same dark chocolate, tall, muscular, well-dressed, good-smelling, perfect-smile-having, confident brutha, so you must be thinking, That sounds like the perfect guy! Where can I find him? And that's exactly what I was thinking: the perfect guy.

The way he looked pulled me in and made me want to know more about him, and of course, I wanted to be with him. I imagined myself boo'd up with him, and I often fantasized about how great our relationship would be. You know you've done that, too! Fate would have it that we had a mutual friend, so we eventually met and started talking. I don't even remember the nature of our first conversation because the voice in my head was screaming, Kiss me! Honestly, I didn't care what he was saying; I just wanted those sexy lips to touch mine. Well, I got my wish, and we kissed and kissed some more (and a very good kisser he was!). That day started our superficial relationship. It didn't take long before I realized I knew nothing about this man's character, his beliefs, his previous lifestyle, or the vision he had for his life. All I knew was we wanted each other physically and nothing else.

About a month later, I sat alone and confused, wondering why I was in a relationship with a man who I felt emotionally and mentally disconnected from. I wondered why this was happening to me again. I realized then that even though he glittered like gold very well, he was not real gold, only fool's gold. Please beware of the delicious eye candy and fool's gold, my friends. Physical attraction has its place in a relationship, and that place should not be first.

Lonely Hearts Club

How many times, as single people, have we felt the sting of loneliness while seeing happy couples during the holidays, on the weekends, at late-night movies, walking through the mall, etc.? Soon after, the painful thoughts of Everybody has somebody except me, the infamous Nobody loves me, and the unforgettable I guess I'll die alone and unmarried start to resonate so loudly in our minds and spirits that we can't focus on the joy of being single and free in that moment. It's this type of infectious thinking that has led many single people to enter relationships under the false pretense of desired togetherness when, actually, they're just tired of being lonely. Just because you're feeling lonely or you're tired of being alone does not mean you are ready to share your life and heart with someone! Come on now, let's get real here; some of you out there don't like yourself enough to spend time with yourself, and you merely want another person in your life to entertain you or keep you company.

Being single is a wonderful gift, just as much as being in a relationship is a gift. Both gifts come with tremendous instructions for maintenance and care. If you need to work on your character, emotional stability, physical fitness, career, education, finances, beliefs, or any other area of your life, this is the time to do it. It is so much easier to improve yourself when you're single versus working on these areas while being in a committed relationship. Having "me time" to reflect and create an environment of peace in your heart, mind, and home will be beneficial for you when you are truly ready to embark on a committed relationship. Once you have learned how to value and appreciate yourself, the right person will cross paths with you at the right time. I'll discuss this more in Chapter 6. (Don't you dare skip ahead!)

During my seasons of singleness, I tried to capitalize on my alone time to self-reflect and self-improve. In my time of self-reflection, I wrote down my thoughts and feelings, no matter how random they were. Just writing them down helped me get the negative feelings out, so my mind and heart could be at peace. Many times, my writings evolved into poetry. In fact, you'll be reading several of those poetry pieces in this book. That poetry came from a place of loneliness, hopelessness, frustration, hurt, and anger, but eventually, it came from a place of forgiveness, peace, love, and satisfaction. During my time of self-improvement, I enrolled in college to further my education, which helped to advance my career and increase my income. Who knew heartbreak and failed relationships would be the fuel to motivate me to earn my bachelor's and master's degrees? I also immersed myself in health and fitness and managed to lose about fifty pounds. Make the most of your single time, and don't succumb to the lure of a temporary relationship due to loneliness.

Approval Ratings

How many times have you been asked the following questions by well-meaning friends, family members, co-workers, or even perfect strangers? "Why are you still single?" "When will you be getting married?" "When will you have kids?" "Did you know your biological clock is ticking?" "How come you haven't found a nice girl/guy yet?" "What are you waiting for? You aren't getting any younger!"

All of these questions and the lack of concrete answers can lead single people to get into relationships for the sake of gaining the approval of those around them. Trying to gain the approval of others will ultimately lead you to rejection and hurt feelings if you end up in a relationship others don't approve of.

I've been through the approval-rejection cycle many times, and it's a complete waste of time, effort, energy, and peace. The best answer to these questions is "When I am ready and the right person for me is ready, we will meet each other at the right time and live happily ever after." Don't surrender to the pressure of getting married and starting a family just because your friends are doing it or because society is pushing a certain standard. You must always keep in mind that you are the CEO of your life; don't hire someone just because those around you think you should. After all, you are the one who will be stuck working with them or, in this case, living with them.

Make it a point to affirm and approve yourself and your decisions every day in some special way, whether you say positive affirmations in the mirror while preparing for your day, treat yourself to lunch or dinner at an upscale restaurant, splurge on a pair of nice shoes or piece of clothing, take a trip to a new destination, or have a spa day. Do whatever it takes to make you feel special and of value; you deserve the best. You are a wonderful gift to the world, and you do not need the approval of others to feel good about yourself!

When you were in middle or high school, peer pressure was always around you; you often felt pressured to conform to the crowd, whether it was the way you wore your hair, what music you listened to, what clothes you wore, or even what slang you used. Approval ratings are the same thing, just in adult form. Either way, don't change your life's path, goals, hopes, or dreams to gain the approval of others. Just because everyone else is doing it doesn't mean you have to join in the crowd. Stand proudly in your singleness as an example of your happiness and self-confidence. Remember, you are living your life for you, not for the approval of those around you!

One of my favorite TV commercials that illustrates this concept is the one by Enterprise Rental Cars. In the commercial, a young lady reserves a rental car over the phone, and a male Enterprise employee comes to her family reunion to pick her up in the rental car, which is a convenient service Enterprise offers. She pretends the Enterprise employee is her new boyfriend, so her well-meaning family will stop nagging her about finding a nice guy. The Enterprise employee catches on quickly to her charade and plays along, then they are able to quickly leave the family reunion together in the rental car. It's apparent to me that this young lady was happy being single and whole, while her relatives continued to apply the pressure of marriage and relationships on her. She went to great lengths to avoid that pressure at the family reunion by introducing her fake boyfriend, the Enterprise male employee, and quickly leaving. Although this is a cute commercial with a funny ending, I'm certain that many of you are actually going through this and are probably quite frustrated and annoyed with the constant nagging from others. It is my hope that after you have finished reading this book, you will feel happy and whole and gain the tools necessary to counter any peer pressure and/or approval rating tactics that will certainly come your way. *Remember, you are enough!*

Judgement Day

You must stop sentencing yourself to a lifetime punishment of bad relationships. You have made yourself the judge, jury, and prosecuting attorney of your past relationships, and you have found yourself guilty as charged. What do I mean by this, you ask? I'll explain. Just because you made a few bad relationship choices in the past doesn't mean you have to continue making those same poor choices. Sometimes we just don't see the signs that someone isn't a good fit for us, so we proceed with the relationship, only to get hurt in the end. The goal of any bad breakup is to learn what you did wrong and try to never do those things again. The worst thing you can do is repeatedly make the same mistakes and not learn from them.

This particular topic hits home for me. I have been married and divorced twice, and believe it or not, I married the same type of man each time. At the time, I was completely unaware because I had not processed the circumstances surrounding the demise of my first marriage, and therefore, I repeated the same mistakes in my second marriage. To add insult to injury, I was my second spouse's third wife, and he, too, had not properly assessed nor healed from the demise of his first two marriages. We created a situation where two broken people were trying to become one, and that is a recipe for disaster.

This is the type of relationship behavior pattern that lands many of us in places of defeat. I literally sentenced myself to a second bad marriage and, consequently, a second divorce. After the second divorce, I forced myself to really examine myself and my situation to find out what I was doing wrong to end up in the same place again. I came to a few conclusions over the course of five years, and I will discuss those conclusions with you as we dive into the next few chapters. My goal is to help you open your eyes sooner than mine were and give you the tools to identify those patterns of behavior and thinking that are leading you to make the same bad relationship choices. It's time to use better judgement to acquire the relationships we deserve and desire.

Religious Rights

Some of you may have found yourself in a bad relationship because of your religion's stance on marriage and dating. Now, let me say this up front; I'm not here to interpret any religious beliefs as better or worse than another. I will only attempt to highlight a pattern of decision-making concerning religious beliefs and relationships. With that being said, I can certainly identify with those of you who have made the choice to be in a relationship because of the expectations of those in your religious group.

As a child, I was brought up in a Christian home and was taught to not engage in sexual activities before marriage because it was a gift from God. Practicing abstinence was expected of me, and I held on tightly to that virtue, which led me to marriage at a very young age—nineteen years old to be exact. I didn't want to disappoint God and my family by having sex outside of marriage, so it was in my best interest to marry the young man that ignited my teenage passions. We married, had three wonderful sons, and divorced after seven years together. We assumed that our religious beliefs were all we needed to have a successful marriage. Conversely, our religious beliefs were all we had in common; we didn't have the same goals, focus, likes, or support system in place to establish a firm foundation for a happy, stable marriage. Our divorce was hard and painful for both of us, as well as our children. I don't blame my religious beliefs, but I do understand that compatibility is needed in more than just one area for a relationship to be successful.

Some of you may be in a situation where your future mate has been arranged or preselected for you. I've never personally been in this type of relationship before; however, based on my personal observations of arranged couples, some fare very well together, while others do not. I can only imagine the loneliness, horror, and disgust that can come from being married to someone you simply do not like and did not choose. I assume those feelings are similar to mine and everyone else's who have been in relationships with mates they chose but didn't connect with.

Following your religious beliefs and convictions is a very serious matter and should not be taken lightly. Marriage and relationships are equally very serious matters that will affect every area of your life. I encourage you to search deeply into your heart, mind, and spirit when choosing a mate based on your religious preferences. Having the same religious beliefs is certainly not a guarantee for happiness but rather one piece in the beautiful puzzle we call love.

Financial Fantasy

When I think about money and financial matters, all I

can hear are the famous bass cords of the electric guitar and the melodious voices of The O'Jays singing, "Money, money, money, money, money!"1 There have been many other songs written about how money and relationships affect one another, but The O'Jays' "For the Love of Money" is one of my favorites. Entangling romance and finance has gotten many couples in trouble over the years, possibly even you; let's talk about it.

Many times, singles get into relationships because they are going through a financial rough patch. Just because you are going through some temporary financial difficulty does not mean you are ready to be in a committed relationship; actually, the opposite is true. Starting a relationship in a financial deficit is the worst possible position you can put yourself in. Why would you want to do that? Even though we live in a culture where having a sugar daddy/sugar momma or being a sugar baby is openly celebrated by many, you can't conclude that this relationship choice is a good one. Look at it this way: Once your partner figures out you are just there for the money and financial benefits, they will drop you—hard! And once you have been dropped, aren't you right back in the same financial position you were in before that relationship?

You are so much better than being a gold digger. You have the ability to gain control over your finances, so you won't feel compelled to rely on others for a comfortable life. You don't need to have the financial know-how of a Wall Street stock broker to manage your finances well. One helpful thing I started doing when I began struggling financially years ago was buying a blank notebook and writing down my budget. (I still do this today, but instead of using notebook paper, I use a digital spreadsheet.) I realized I didn't know where my paychecks were going, and I'd have more month than money, so I needed to physically see where my money was being spent. Writing down the amount of my paycheck (income) then writing down the name of my bills, their due dates, and the amounts due (expenses) helped me plan (budget) when I should pay certain bills. After doing this for several months, I was able to see where my money was being spent, where I needed to make lifestyle/spending changes so I wouldn't go over budget, and where I could afford to save and reduce my debt load. I also started educating myself on money management skills by reading books, listening to financial speakers, and putting what I learned to practice.

Having good financial sense as a single person can be a desirable characteristic when you do end up finding the right person or the right person finds you. You won't feel pressured to be with someone for their money, and that person will feel good knowing you are there purely for their love. Being financially stable will give you the confidence you need to avoid making wrong financial and relationship decisions.

Let's Grow from Here!

Now that we have identified the main culprits that keep us in a bad relationship cycle, we are ready to drill down into the nuts and bolts of how to break free from these bad relationship habits and cycles, so we can eventually start healthy and successful ones. If falling for the Eye Candy Appeal, being a member of the Lonely Hearts Club, craving Approval Ratings, repeating Judgement Day, accepting Religious Rights, and being in a Financial Fantasy haven't gotten you into the loving relationship you desire, isn't it time for a major change? We cannot continue to do the same things, think the same thoughts, and speak the same words while expecting a different end result. Sounds like insanity, right? Well, it is! But now that we know better, we are certainly going to do better. Are you ready? I am, so let's grow!

CHAPTER ONE
REFLECTIONS

Have you chosen a partner based on the reasons above? Take a moment to think about this and write down your thoughts. You can even write down the name or initials of the individuals who fit into each category. This will help you identify, clarify, and understand why you made these choices in the past, so you can hopefully avoid repeating them in the future. Be honest with yourself!

EYE CANDY APPEAL:

_____

_____

_____

_____

_____

_____

_____

_____

_____

_____

_____

_____

_____

_____

_____

LONELY HEARTS CLUB:

_____

_____

_____

_____

_____

_____

_____

_____

_____

_____

_____

_____

_____

JUDGEMENT DAY:

_____
_____
_____
_____
_____
_____
_____
_____
_____
_____
_____
_____
_____
_____
_____
_____
_____

RELIGIOUS RIGHTS:

_____
_____
_____
_____

_____
_____
_____
_____
_____
_____
_____
_____
_____
_____
_____

FINANCIAL FANTASY:

_____
_____
_____
_____
_____
_____
_____
_____
_____
_____
_____
_____
_____

_____

_____

IN THE FUTURE, I WILL CHOOSE A PARTNER/SPOUSE BASED ON THESE CHARACTERISTICS:

_____

_____

_____

_____

_____

_____

_____

_____

_____

_____

_____

_____

_____

_____

_____

Signs That It's Time
To Go

Poem: Premonition

"Premonition"

I always knew this day would come, when you'd
pardon yourself from out of my life
To take my heart, to create sudden strife.
I saw, afraid for you to leave.
I was holding on so tight; you're not leaving me
without a fight!
I'll kick, I'll scream, "I love you, man!"
What do you want from me? I'm givin' what I can!
I thought you really wanted to love me.
I was such a fool for you; I know you see!
Wow! How did I know today would be the day?
My premonition paved the way!
I saw you in my dreams, just fade to black
Like a ghostly shadow behind my back.
I felt you so strong, yet I feel nothing now
But anger, sadness, shame—but how?
If I saw this day, then why were you so blind?
Or did you ignore the warning, just to have me
by your side?

That's not fair to waste my time, to waste my love,
to waste my mind!
If you wanted sex, you could get that anywhere!
If you want my love, baby, I'm standing right here!
So look at us now, just staring blankly into space,
Wishing and longing to be in each other's face.
I still want you, still long for you, still need you.
I know you still want me, still long for me,
still need me, too.
The universe will make our paths cross again.
My premonition tells me so, my lover, my friend.
I love you!
Like Maxwell said, "You could've saved me my
fist full of tears"
'Cause I wanted more years.
But all I can do now is hope and wait and run!
Keep watching the moon and praying to the sun
To take away the pain of losing you too soon.
And with my 20/20 hindsight vision, my premonition,
I'll seal my heart with steel to keep you out;
that's my decision!
We've met before in our previous lives,
just different faces in different places
In different phases.
So let's stop repeating the past in our present,
Especially since we can see what's coming in it.
You were me, and I was you; we're one in the same.
How many lifetimes do you want to play this game?
I saw you, and you see me, so hopefully, next lifetime,
we'll be happy!

It's all in how we perceive our premonitions!
—Jeanine Mack, 5/16/2010

2

Chapter 2: Signs That It's Time To Go

Chapter 2: Signs That It's Time to Go

In 2016, I relocated to the beautiful city of Orlando, Florida, to pursue a new career and a new life. I can still remember the anxiety I felt on my first day of work as I embarked on my journey of driving during the infamous morning rush hour traffic. I had just moved from Daytona Beach, Florida, where rush hour traffic would increase my fifteen-minute commute to a twenty- to twenty-five-minute commute; however, in Orlando, a fifteen-minute commute could very easily evolve into an hour-long commute, depending on the road conditions. I desperately wanted to be on time for my first day, so I could make a great first impression. I decided to consult the Google Maps app for the quickest route to work. As Google gave me the turn-by-turn directions, I began to notice various road signs I also had to follow to arrive safely at my workplace. (Side note: I must add, I'm one of those people who can get lost, even when using GPS, so I need all the obvious signs I can get to arrive at my intended destination.)

I noticed there were signs that let me know when a toll plaza was coming up and which lane to use to get there. There was a huge electronic sign that told me there was going to be congestion ahead for the next three miles due to an accident. There were signs warning me about speed limit reductions and road construction, signs to let me know if I was heading north, south, east, or west, signs for the exits to theme parks, eateries, outlet malls, etc. And finally, after reading all the road signs and listening to my Google Maps app, I arrived at my new job in the nick of time. After a week, I no longer needed my Google Maps app, nor did I read the road signs because I successfully learned which way to go.

Likewise, in relationships, we often need signs to tell us when it's safe to proceed in a relationship and when it's time to exit. In this chapter, we will focus on those obvious and not-so-obvious signs of when it's time to exit a bad relationship. If we are honest with ourselves, the signs of a bad relationship are always there, but we choose to ignore them. So, just like how I needed Google Maps and the road signs to get to work, some of you need this book to help you identify the safest path out of a bad relationship. Please allow me to be your Google Maps guide to get you where you need to be in your relationships. Some of you may need to read this book a few times until you have learned the signs so well you can begin to avoid bad relationships altogether. I want you to live a happy, healthy, and whole life and experience nothing but positive relationships.

The Signs Revealed

After each one of my breakups, I reflected on the reasons why the relationship failed. During my time of reflection, I always seemed to recognize the signs I couldn't see in the beginning of the relationship, signs that would've given me a red flag that trouble would ensue. Have you heard the old cliché, "Hindsight is 20/20"? Of course, I, like many others, elected to ignore those signs and the preceding signs for one or all of the reasons we discussed in Chapter 1. Let's take a deeper look at the warning signs that tell us when a relationship is over and, ultimately, when it's time to move on.

These signs are not listed in any particular order; they just happen at will and can be a reason your relationships fail.

•*Lack of Interest:* A lack of interest includes a lack of dating in your relationship, not caring about how or what the other person is doing/feeling, or choosing to be isolated instead of together like you used to be.

•*Communication Breakdown:* Remember when you and your partner would text each other first thing in the morning and right before bed? Now, there are no texts all day, and you're wondering why. The long phone calls where you talked about everything and nothing at all have now ceased. You eat dinner in silence and subject each other to the silent treatment instead of engaging in conversation. You avoid face-to-face interaction at all costs.

• *The Thrill Is Gone:* You know the thrill is gone when you no longer feel an attraction to the other person, whether physically or emotionally. Those butterflies in your stomach are gone, and the tingles you once felt have transformed into dread and hate. You feel unloved, unwanted, unappreciated, disrespected, annoyed, and even angry. Your sexual relationship has decreased or is nonexistent, and you loathe the thought of sexually gratifying your partner. Emotional and mental intimacy is no longer present, and that inner connection you once had is now detached.

• *I'm Number One:* You used to make the other person a priority in your life, and now, anything and everything, such as work, family, friends, hobbies, sleep, and your own wants and needs, take precedence over your partner. You overvalue and demand your "me time" instead of focusing on "we time."

• *Fears and Speculation:* The fear of being replaced has crept into the relationship, which leads to mistrust, verbal and physical abuse, accusations of infidelity, sneaky and questionable behavior, stalking, or irrational thoughts and behavior.

Based on the signals above and thinking about your present relationship, do you see yellow flags of caution or red flags that tell you to stop immediately? Any type of sign from this list should not be ignored nor taken lightly. These are not good signs, whether you are on the giving or receiving end of such behaviors. You should seriously consider if you want to continue in your current relationship if you notice any of these patterns. Most relationships are repairable if both partners are willing to put in the work, but if only one is willing to put in the effort, the relationship simply will not last. In the words of hip-hop duo Rob Base & DJ E-Z Rock, "It takes two to make a thing go right!"

Please seek professional counseling to assist you with healing strategies that can repair your relationship. I can recall going to marriage counseling at the end of my first marriage—again, at the end, not the beginning or middle, which would have been the best time to go. Unfortunately, we waited too long, and there was a lot of pain and turmoil within the marriage that seemed irreparable at the time. We were young and impatient with the healing process and, therefore, chose to live separately for two years while hurting. Finally, we made our separation permanent with a divorce. Our three sons were the casualties of our marital war. Years later, I realized he and I never restored ourselves completely, which led us both to remarry, only to divorce again.

Signs for Better Days Ahead

If you have already exited your relationship and can now see the signs that were there, please remember them, so you don't make the same mistakes again. Making mistakes is a part of life; however, learning from them is a sign of maturity. So don't beat yourself up about it; just learn and move forward with healing. We've all been there, and I certainly have been there more than I'd like to admit. I'm a sucker for romance, and that character trait has gotten me in relationship trouble many times. Take the time to reflect, acknowledge your part, heal, and begin again. Also, seek professional counseling, so you can learn some helpful methods to heal your broken heart, mind, and spirit.

CHAPTER TWO
REFLECTIONS

What signs from this chapter have you noticed in your current or past relationships?

_____

_____

_____

_____

_____

_____

_____

_____

_____

What steps will you take in the future to ensure you recognize these signs?

_____

_____

_____

_____

_____

_____

_____

_____

_____

_____

_____

_____

_____

If There's Abuse, It's No Use

Poem: When Love Turns to Hate

"When Love Turns to Hate"

When love turns to hate, there's no more dates; you exacerbate. I dare to create, refuse to elate, collate my state of mind...Satan, get thee behind!

When love turns to hate, things explode, go out of control, my heart implodes, burn the dinner rolls, this is how I roll and stroll!

When love turns to hate, there's nothing you can say to make my day, get on your way, complain. I may, look for ships in the bay, decide not to stay, there's gotta be a better way...to say goodbye.

When love turns to hate, it's the worst feeling in the world, to see your face and want to hurl, to ball up in a curl, to settle for kissing girls, go diving for pearls inside my dark world...and wonder where did we go wrong?

I used to turn to you for love, but not anymore.

—Jeanine Mack, 6/17/10

3

Chapter 3: If there's Abuse, It's No Use

Chapter 3: If There's Abuse, It's No Use

Abuse in relationships is a very serious matter. It should not be taken lightly nor excused or accepted. Abuse can take on several forms: mental, emotional, verbal, spiritual, and physical, to name a few. Before healing your heart from abuse, you must understand exactly what abuse is, so you can (a) recognize the early signs of it and, ultimately, keep it from happening to you and (b) ensure you are not exhibiting abusive behaviors that will lead to the demise of any relationship you seek in the future.

According to the Merriam-Webster Online Dictionary2, "abuse" is defined as follows:

Abuse (Noun):

•a corrupt practice or custom

•improper or excessive use or treatment: misuse

- language that condemns or vilifies usually unjustly, intemperately, and angrily
- physical maltreatment
- obsolete: a deceitful act: deception

Abuse (Verb):

- a: to put to a wrong or improper use
- b: to use excessively; also: to use without medical justification
- to use or treat so as to injure or damage: maltreat
- to attack in words: revile
- obsolete: deceive

Now that we have correctly defined the word "abuse," can you determine if abuse has been present in your current or past relationships? Are you an abuser? Let's be honest here; real, unconditional love does not operate within abuse. Those are two opposing forces and should never be viewed as equal nor as being intertwined. I think this is a great segue to define the word "love." Even though we all may think we know what love really is, let's view it from the perspective of scholars. "Love" is defined as follows, according to Dictionary.com3:

Love (Noun):

- a profoundly tender, passionate affection for another person
- a feeling of warm personal attachment or deep affection, as for a parent, child, or friend
- sexual passion or desire
- a person toward whom love is felt; beloved person; sweetheart

- used in direct address as a term of endearment, affection, or the like
- a love affair; an intensely amorous incident; amour
- sexual intercourse; copulation

Love (Verb):
- to have love or affection for
- to have a profoundly tender, passionate affection for (another person)
- to have a strong liking for; take great pleasure in
- to need or require; benefit greatly from
- to embrace and kiss (someone), as a lover
- to have sexual intercourse with
- to have love or affection for another person; be in love

As we can clearly see, "abuse" and "love" have entirely different definitions and applications. These terms are not to be used synonymously or interchangeably. To put it bluntly, abuse and love are not the same thing! From these definitions above, please ask yourself, which one do you prefer to have an abundance of in your relationship? Of course, you will say love; however, my personal experience and observations of others tell me quite the opposite. You deserve to be loved unconditionally and completely. If your partner does not love you according to the definitions of love above and you are experiencing the definitions of abuse instead, it's time to reconsider the future of that relationship. Like I said before, "You are the CEO of your life; hire and fire accordingly!" You are the gatekeeper of your life, too. You don't have to open your gates to everyone who wants to enter your life; you can say no and go.

Abuse by the Numbers

The occurrence of abuse within relationships has increased at an alarming rate over the past few years. The following statistics have been reported by the National Coalition Against Domestic Violence4, and these numbers were very surprising. It occurred to me that so many people continue to hurt and suffer in silence. Let's review the numbers to gain a better perspective.

•On average, nearly twenty people are physically abused by an intimate partner every minute in the United States. Over the course of one year, this equates to more than 10 million women and men.

•One in three women and one in four men have been victims of [some form of] physical violence by an intimate partner within their lifetime.

•One in four women and one in seven men have been victims of severe physical violence by an intimate partner in their lifetime.

•On a typical day, there are more than 20,000 phone calls placed to domestic violence hotlines nationwide.

•The presence of a gun in a domestic violence situation increases the risk of homicide by 500%.

•Intimate partner violence accounts for 15% of all violent crimes.

With these staggering statistics in mind, what can you do to ensure you do not become one of these statistics? Remove yourself from the relationship. And yes, it is just that simple.

Don't complicate the decision to save yourself, your children, family, or friends from becoming a statistic. In Chapter 5, I will outline a brief strategy on how to remove yourself from a toxic relationship.

What can you do if you have a friend or loved one who is currently experiencing abuse? You don't have to turn a blind eye any longer. It is your business, and you do have a voice. You can certainly be an advocate for the voiceless, even if that voice is anonymous to the local authorities and abuse hotlines. Whatever you decide to do to help, just please decide to do something! I've had the opportunity to be an advocate for the voiceless, and it's not an easy task; however, the alternative was losing my friends forever, and I certainly did not want that to happen.

One of my friends found herself in an abusive relationship with her "dream guy," and she remained in that relationship for six long and fearful years. She constantly made excuses for the frequent beatings she received from him, such as "He only beats me up when he drinks and does drugs," "I really love him; he just needs help," "No one else will help him if I don't," "I'm the only one who understands him," "We make a really good couple," and "He's a great guy and provider." Never mind her several broken bones, her swollen face, her damaged self-esteem and self-confidence, the terror and fear he made her live with, and the life he nearly took from her!

One day, she woke up physically, mentally, spiritually, and emotionally and decided she wanted to live her life without the abuse. She gathered her clothes and a few possessions and moved away. That was a bold step for her, and with the support of her family and friends, she's making the biggest comeback of her life. She can now be the type of loving mother, better friend, great employee, and healthy woman she always saw herself becoming.

The Resolution

This is the ugly side of domestic violence and abuse; however, the good news is you can decide today to stop being a statistic. You are more valuable to this world than you probably believe. You have an abundance of untapped potential that this world needs. If you are the abusive person in the relationship, you, too, can decide today to stop being a statistic. I have provided a list of organizations and other resources at the end of this book. These groups are ready and willing to help you in your next step toward ending the cycle of abuse in your life. Please take advantage of these resources, so you can regain your life and start loving yourself the way your Creator intended.

As I stated at the beginning of this chapter, abuse and love have two very different definitions and expressions. They should never be thought of, spoken of, or acted upon as the same. Love is not present within abuse, and abuse cannot exist when love is present. Remember, you are the CEO of your life; hire and fire accordingly. You are the gatekeeper of your life, as well. You don't have to open your gates to everyone who wants to enter your life; you can say no and go. Make a boss move today. My friend did it, and so can you!

CHAPTER THREE
REFLECTIONS

How do you define love? Give examples of how you show love to yourself and others.

_____

_____

_____

_____

_____

_____

_____

_____

_____

_____

_____

_____

_____

_____

How do you define abuse? Have you experienced any type of abuse?

_____

_____

_____

_____

_____

_____

_____

_____

_____

_____

—

What action steps will you take in the future to ensure you don't become an abuser or a victim of abuse?

_____

_____

_____

_____

_____

_____

_____

_____

_____

_____

_____

_____

The Break-Up Strategy

Poem: The Rising

"The Rising"

Every event happens in seasons;
Everything happens for a reason,
But I'm rising…
I now hate the taste of dust and dirt,
Living day to day, rehearsing my hurt,
But I'm rising…
My wings were clipped, and I was caged in my sin.
The Capturer is dead; he no longer lives within,
So I'm rising…
Just like the cracked egg reveals its yolk,
My broken spirit has revealed some hope,
So I'm rising…
It's time to break free of the misery called me;
It's time to get back on track and wash my feet.
I'm stepping to my original beat
Because I'm rising…
I'll keep reaching toward the Son of Man,
Basking in His sunlight; He takes my hand,
So I can rise…
My spirit is free, my mind is released,

my heart repaired,
No longer ensnared…
I have risen!
—Jeanine Mack, 8/28/10

4

Chapter 4: The Break Up Strategy

Chapter 4: The Break Up Strategy

Now that we have identified the areas of our lives that have led us to choose the wrong people for our relationships, recognized the signs that it's time to exit a bad relationship, and lastly, acknowledged the abuse and love dichotomies, we are ready to take on the task of actually breaking up! Like any other successful venture, you must have a plan in place before beginning. I'd like to introduce what I call The Break Up Strategy, a.k.a The BUS. It's time for you to get on The BUS, so the rest of your life can be the best of your life.

Now, there are several relationship scenarios I will discuss because there are several relationship situations and issues that can arise. I'll focus on the most prevalent ones to keep my Break Up Strategy easy to understand and follow.

The Break Up Strategy (The BUS)

Scenario One

Kevin and Tameka have been married for five years and have two small children together. At Kevin's request, Tameka quit her job to be a stay-at-home mom. As a result, Kevin constantly yells at Tameka and calls her names because she doesn't contribute financially to their household. He also tells her she is unattractive because she no longer wears makeup nor does she dress up like she used to before having children. Kevin has begun spending time away from Tameka and their children to pursue an extramarital affair with a woman from his office. Tameka found out about Kevin's affair after reading a text from the woman on Kevin's phone. Tameka has finally decided she can no longer remain in her marriage, and she wants out but doesn't know what to do. Tameka should do the following:

• She should try to talk with Kevin about the text message she saw on his phone. This can be tough to do since emotions are running high and getting revenge is probably her foremost thought. Giving Kevin the opportunity to explain the text and his relationship will be key in her decision-making concerning the future of their marriage. She should suggest they go to a counselor for help because an uninvolved third party can help couples get to the root of their problems.

• If the marriage is not salvageable after talking and counseling, Tameka needs to start preparing herself to reenter the job market. She will need income to support herself and her children, even though she may receive child support and alimony from the divorce. She understands those matters will be resolved at a future date, and she needs to generate income now. She should ask friends and family to babysit while she applies for jobs and goes on interviews, and she should acquire a few professional outfits to help her look her best and feel confident.

•Tameka and Kevin will have to work out a co-parenting arrangement for their children. Often, the biggest casualties in a divorce are the children. Despite the couple's negative feelings toward each other, their children should be their highest priority.

•Lastly, Tameka will need to consult legal advice concerning the dissolution of her marriage. Getting a divorce is never an easy decision when it's time to actually draft the documents and come to the realization that your once happily-ever-after is now your worst nightmare.

Scenario Two

Rosie and Juan have been dating for six months, and they post every outing they take together on their social media accounts. They are the perfect fantasy couple—physically fit bodies, great fashion, gorgeous looks, awesome destination trips, and lots of adoring friends—when they are on social media. Outside of social media, in their real lives, Juan feels like a piece of meat, a tool, and a possession of Rosie's social media life. He realizes they have nothing in common other than being two attractive people with a lot of followers on social media. Juan now sees that this is not a real relationship, and he wants to end things with Rosie. He fears she will retaliate with harmful posts on her social media accounts. Juan should do the following:

•He should talk to Rosie face-to-face about his thoughts and feelings regarding their relationship and gently let her know that he is only interested in being friends moving forward.

•Juan needs to unfollow, untag, and unfriend Rosie on all of his social media accounts and ask her to do the same. He should also remove all posts that have Rosie in them, so it is clear to their friends and followers that they are no longer a couple. This will also give Juan the opportunity to become a separate entity from Rosie in the social media world.

•If Juan finds out that Rosie is posting negative things about him on social media, he should promptly contact the customer service advocates for the platform to have the harmful posts removed.

•In the world of social media and the internet, a breakup can become very public very fast, so it's important to be aware of what you post on social media because it can be next to impossible to remove the content once it's out there in cyberspace. And this is true for everyone, from the rich and famous to the poor and unknown. Social media, and the laws that govern it, are still new and uncharted territory we don't usually think about until we want to remove content. Please post wisely, my friends.

Scenario Three

Cameron and Isis are both separated from their soon-to-be ex-spouses and have divorces pending. In the meantime, they have found solace in one another. During the weekends their children are with their spouses, they make a point to spend time together, go on dates, and stay over at each other's apartments. They text and talk to each other daily about work, their exes, their families, and anything else that arises; however, after a few months into the relationship, Isis notices that Cameron has started to exhibit the same personality traits her ex-husband did, which contributed to the demise of their marriage. In the spirit of friendship, Isis decided to talk to Cameron about her concerns regarding his behavior. Cameron confessed that he is who he is and that Isis sometimes reminds him of his demanding mother. Stunned by these revelations, Cameron started to withdraw from Isis and eventually told her they should just be friends and stop seeing each other. Even though Isis didn't like his suggestion, she agreed.

After eight months of not speaking to one another, Cameron texted Isis and asked for a date. Isis quickly fell back into the routine of their prior relationship, and again, Cameron's behavior began to mirror her ex-husband's. This time, Isis decided she no longer wanted a relationship with Cameron because he was her ex-husband reincarnated. Isis is now struggling with her decision because Cameron is a great lover in the bedroom but quite a jerk outside of it. Isis should do the following:

•She should stop engaging in sexual contact with Cameron immediately. Engaging in further sexual contact with him only complicates their breakup. When we have sexual contact with someone, soul ties are developed. Soul ties are great when you are in a solid, committed relationship, but they're bad for short-term, non-committed relationships. The pain we feel inside when leaving our lovers is real. Please don't underestimate the power of sex.

• Isis should speak with Cameron again about how his behavior makes her feel, and she should tell him in clear terms that this time their relationship is truly over. After the first breakup, she knew what she was getting back into, and she shouldn't have expected anything different from Cameron.

•Isis needs to focus her time and energy on rebuilding herself by paying close attention to the needs of her children and the tasks of finalizing her divorce.

•She must realize that until she gets to the root causes of her failed marriage, she will continue to repeat those same patterns in her future relationships.

Scenario Four

Max and Ybeth have been married for a few months but have been a couple for seven years. Ybeth's friend Carolisa has noticed that Ybeth has become more and more withdrawn from her friends and family with each year she's in a relationship with Max; she's even stopped using a cellphone. One day, Carolisa bumped into Ybeth at the local grocery store and barely recognized her. She was frail and thin and wore large shades to cover her two blackened eyes. When asked about her appearance, Ybeth insisted she was on a strict diet that caused her drastic weight loss, and she fell off a treadmill at the gym, which caused her blackened eyes. Carolisa is concerned that her friend is being isolated and abused by her husband. If Ybeth is truly being abused by Max, she should do the following:

• Ybeth is not in a position to do anything to help herself; she doesn't have a cellphone to make a call for help, and she is being isolated from her friends and family. She is probably too afraid and embarrassed to reach out to anyone.

• Carolisa can help her friend by contacting a domestic abuse center or calling a domestic abuse hotline for information and tips on how to best help Ybeth.

• Carolisa, along with Ybeth's other friends and family members, can provide a safe haven for Ybeth to heal and rebuild her life after she has left her marriage with Max.

• Ybeth should strongly consider involving the police and having Max charged with domestic violence.

Scenario Five

Alexandria and Derek have found themselves in a new, hot romance that seemed to have blossomed overnight. There's only one major problem in their newfound relationship: Alexandria is Derek's supervisor at work. They are both well aware their company's policy prohibits supervisors and subordinates from engaging in romantic relationships, whether inside or outside the workplace. Alexandria could be fired immediately if the romance was revealed to upper management. Three months into their relationship, the human resources (HR) manager met with Alexandria to discuss Derek's excessive tardiness and unapproved overtime and wanted to know why she had not written him up for it per company policy. The HR manager also told Alexandria that an anonymous tip was received, stating she was showing favoritism to Derek by giving him the best work assignments. Alexandria is now being considered for a write-up, demotion, or possible termination from the company. Alexandria should take the following steps:

- Alexandria needs to have a serious conversation with Derek outside of the workplace to discuss how their relationship is affecting her job. She needs to be honest and tell him that his tardiness and unapproved overtime will result in a write-up moving forward.

- Derek needs to admit he has taken advantage of their relationship within the workplace and bragged about it to one of his co-workers. He also needs to apologize to Alexandria for jeopardizing her job.

- Alexandria needs to explain to Derek that it was a mistake to break the company's policy and that she is ending their relationship to protect her employment.

- Alexandria should also speak to the HR manager and admit to her relationship with Derek and the favoritism she showed him. She should also recommend that Derek be transferred to a different supervisor to ensure he will receive the same treatment as the other employees. In doing this, Alexandria can possibly salvage both her and Derek's jobs.

Now, you may be wondering why my BUS doesn't involve slashing tires, busting car windows with a baseball bat, burning clothes, posting disrespectful memes on social media, or all of the other crazy and, oftentimes, dangerous revenge activities you've probably done, seen, or heard people do. Well, I never advise anyone to engage in illegal or socially disruptive behavior just because their heart has been broken. Listen, we entered these bad relationships as adults, not high school students; therefore, we need to exit them as such. As tempting as it is to call your best friend or relative to ride with you across town to bust Jimmy's windshield on his beloved sports car, please don't give in to that temptation. Jimmy isn't worth it! Revenge and anger are normal feelings, but what separates adults from teenagers is the way in which you manage those emotions.

You may see a part or all of yourself in any of those five scenarios, or your situation may be a hybrid of a few of them. Whatever your situation may be, there is a way out if you truly want to get on The BUS. I didn't give examples of every type of relationship possible, but these are the most popular relationship adversities I encounter. My hope is that, as you read those scenarios, you gained helpful insight on how to break up and move forward with your life. Sometimes just knowing that others have gone through what you are going through and are now living well is enough motivation to help you make the decision to start living a better life, too.

As you can see from these five scenarios, The BUS can be a challenge to follow, but it starts with a decision to break free from negativity and drama. The BUS is always there waiting for you, but you have to choose to strive for a better love life for yourself. You were created for love, abundance, and a good life, and being a part of broken, loveless, and abusive relationships is not going to produce the beautiful life you desire. Don't delay any further. Make the choice to get on The BUS today!

CHAPTER FOUR
REFLECTIONS

Which of the above scenarios can you identify with the most, and why?

_____

_____

_____

_____

_____

_____

_____

_____

_____

_____

_____

_____

_____

_____

_____

_____

_____

_____

_____

How did you handle your most recent breakup?

_____

_____

_____

_____

_____

_____

_____

_____

_____

_____

_____

What could you have done differently to initiate your last breakup, or if you were on the receiving end, was your reaction destructive or constructive?

_____

_____

_____

_____

_____

_____

_____

_____

_____

_____

_____

_____

_____

Based on the advice shared in this chapter, what have you learned about the way you deal with heartbreak, disappointment, and breakups?

_____

_____

_____

_____

_____

_____

_____

_____

_____

_____

_____

The Ultimate
Break-Up: YOU!

Poem: Mirror, Mirror...

"Mirror, Mirror..."

I wish I could see a different version of me, but what
I see is my reflection of defeat.
How could so much success come to this?
The greatness, the goals, the wins…it's all amiss!
In one fateful decision, my rise became a fall,
and I lost it all.
As I drift then drown in my own tears of sorrow,
It's my hopes and dreams and love from the past
I wish to borrow. No hope for tomorrow!
But no, not a chance! Because it's you that I must
look upon and glance.
Just a mere shadow of golden sunsets past,
which are morphed into my present ghosts.
My pride and ego had me out here doing the most;
how dare I boast!
Oh mirror, mirror, if only you could see that there
is still some worth left inside of me!
I desire to change, but these shackles got me

so weighted down in misery.

Oh my God, please save me! There's got to be
more for me!

Today, I reflect defeat, but tomorrow,

I'm gonna march to a new beat!

Just watch me, mirror. I'm gonna change…I'm gonna
change…I'm gonna change.

—Jeanine Mack, 7/23/18

5

Chapter 5: The Ultimate Breakup - YOU!

Chapter 5: The Ultimate Breakup: You!

In this chapter, we're going to focus on the most important breakup you'll experience: the breakup with yourself. Yes, you read that correctly, my friend. You have to break up with yourself! Now is the time to take responsibility for your part in staying in toxic relationships, entertaining shenanigans, and checking in on exes and other destructive people. In the previous chapters, we focused on the external reasons of how and why we often end up in bad relationships, but in this chapter, we are going to focus on the internal factors that contribute to those unproductive relationships forming in the first place. Are you ready? Let's dive into the deep end of the pool, which is you!

Your Thoughts Have Tricked You!

I've been told that the most powerful force we possess is located right between our ears: our brain. Well, what's inside your brain? Your thoughts! And they have the power to either propel you to the highest levels of success or dismantle and diminish your very existence. Both positive and negative thoughts bombard our minds every second of the day, so our success comes down to which thoughts we choose to pay attention to, speak about, and act upon.

Negative thoughts often cause us to lose sleep at night, and in some instances, they even cause nightmares. They make us worry about things that have never happened, see ourselves as worthless—which lowers our self-esteem—convince us to give up on our goals, lose hope, and make bad financial choices, and they can even cause us to choose the wrong relationships. Sometimes negative thoughts enter our minds subconsciously through the TV commercials we watch, the music we listen to, or the magazine ads we see. We end up comparing ourselves to the people we see in our daily lives and what we view on social media platforms. I can recall countless times when I've scrolled through my social media feeds and saw exciting posts of my friends or followers having a great time on vacation, showing off a new car, or snuggling up with a new lover. Even though I was consciously happy for them, I ultimately felt down, defeated, envious, unworthy, and even slightly depressed when I closed the app. Why? Because I was comparing my situation to theirs while thinking one of the following: How come nothing good ever happens to me? Why is it so hard for me to find love? I'll never have enough money to take a nice vacation. If I never had kids, I'd have a flat stomach like the women in the clothing ads. It's so sad to know that so many of us have allowed negative thoughts like these to control the tempo of our lives for so long.

The good news is all hope is not lost. Every day, we can choose to allow positive thoughts to have access to our minds. I know the term "positive thinking" has become so cliché these days, but I can't deny the value that positive thinking brings to our lives. Positive thoughts work conversely to negative thoughts by increasing your self-esteem and self-worth, helping you create strategic plans of your dreams and goals, sparking your hope for the future, inducing pleasant dreams at night, decreasing your worry and stress levels, and keeping you from making bad decisions in your relationships.

Just take a moment to close your eyes and think about lying on a soft, comfy towel on a beautiful, secluded Caribbean beach. The warm, honey-dipped sun caresses your skin, while the cool ocean breeze gently blows through the palm trees nearby. You inhale the scent of tropical flowers and the fresh ocean air, and you hear the distant squawking of seagulls and the chirping of exotic birds in the distance, which lull you to sleep. Did you get a visual of yourself relaxing on this exotic beach? With this little exercise, I've illustrated the power of positive thinking. You can essentially think your way into a good mood, into losing weight, into going after your goals and dreams, and becoming a well-balanced person, so you can become the person you'd like to be while in a relationship. If you are having a bad day, think a positive thought. Don't continue to dwell on the things that cause you stress. Replaying those negative thoughts will steal your joy, sap your physical strength, emotionally drain you, and bring self-doubt instead of self-confidence.

Emotional Rollercoaster

Now, let's talk about our emotions. Our emotions are another culprit that can cause us to make either good or bad decisions when choosing partners for our relationships. Allow me to further dissect this matter. In a recent article published on Forbes.com, Svetlana Whitener stated that "...emotions influence, skew or sometimes completely determine the outcome of a large number of decisions we are confronted with in a day. Therefore, it behooves all of us who want to make the best, most objective decisions to know all we can about emotions and their effect on our decision-making."5 With this information in mind, you can now understand that our decisions are never free from our emotions, even if we feel emotionless. That, too, is an emotion that can impact our decisions.

Some of us are more naturally prone to certain emotions than others, which could be linked to our personality types and emotional predispositions. For example, I tend to be a more emotionally upbeat and happy person, which causes me to make decisions that will hopefully lead to a desirable outcome. However, I have friends and relatives who are more prone to being emotionally quick-tempered and angry, which causes them to make quick, rash decisions that lead to an unwanted, often messy, ending. To be completely honest with you, I wasn't always happy, and I battled feelings of anger because of my circumstances. I used to make bad decisions based on those negative emotions, then wondered why I kept ending up with unhappy conclusions. This is why we need to be watchmen over our hearts and feelings, so we are constantly making a conscious effort to keep our emotions balanced when making our decisions.

Invaluable Self-Worth

How valuable are you to yourself? What value have you placed on yourself? Do you know your self-worth? Do you understand what valuing yourself means? If you don't know the answers to these questions or if you are unsure about the answers, you may be having trouble with your self-image. No one can determine your value and your self-worth; only you can do that. Let's explore this!

In order to know our value, we need to define what value actually is. According to Dictionary.com, value is defined as follows when being used as a verb: to consider with respect to worth, excellence, usefulness, or importance; to regard or esteem highly.

I have a career background in real estate sales. When one of my clients was in the process of closing on their new home, their mortgage provider required them to have an appraisal of the home done to determine its value before the mortgage could be approved. Likewise, in our lives, we need to have a means to measure our value and self-worth. The means cannot be a comparison to those around you, like friends, strangers you see on social media, movie stars, entertainers, etc. You must only measure your value against yourself. It's you versus you! Nobody can beat you at being you; nobody can talk the way you talk; nobody can do anything the same way you do it because God truly broke the mold when He made you. I know that sounds cliché, but take a moment to soak it in and, for once, bask in your uniqueness.

"You versus you" is a competition where you set goals for yourself and accomplish them. In doing this, you will be able to measure your growth in those areas of your life. For example, I set three goals for myself at the age of thirty-five that I wanted to complete by the time I turned forty. One of those goals was to complete my master's degree program. It took me three years and a couple of setbacks, but I was able to complete that goal by the age of forty. I was very proud of myself for accomplishing my goal in the timeframe I set and for overcoming the challenges I faced to get there. The personal, emotional, and mental growth I experienced made me a stronger person than I was when I began goal-setting. My self-worth, value, and self-esteem were through the ceiling on commencement day as I walked across the stage to receive my hood and degree. It didn't matter what anybody else thought about me because I was proud of myself. I placed positive value on myself by engaging in activities that increased my self-worth and value. I competed against myself and won, and in the process, I became a better version of myself.

I Believe in Myself!

Believing in yourself is a major part of becoming the person you want to become. Say this out loud right now, "I believe in myself! I believe in myself! I believe in myself!" Saying it out loud will allow you to hear the words from your own mouth. Self-affirmations are a powerful tool in establishing a healthy self-image and building your self-esteem. By the end of this book, you will be shouting that affirmation from the mountaintops because you will finally see and understand that you are the key—the missing link—to your better self. You have to believe it; you have to get comfortable knowing it, thinking it, feeling it, and living with that mindset every single day for the rest of your life.

So here's where the tough part comes into play when you start believing in yourself: Other people are going to notice this new, more confident version of you, and some of them are not going to like you. But guess what? You are not going to care who likes you or who doesn't because you are going to focus your energy on becoming a better you. You don't need permission to do that, and you will not be apologizing for it, either. You have lived based on the opinions of others long enough, and now it's time for you to serve yourself. Does that sound selfish or harsh? Yes? Good! I really want to make my point that when you break up with the old you, the people around you may not be ready to do the same. They may want the old you back, but that's not an option, so you must stay focused and keep developing the new you. Eventually, they will adjust, or they just won't have a seat at the table in your life. Period!

Now I must add that you will have days or moments when you won't feel like you believe in yourself. You will have doubts, and that's normal. We've all been preconditioned to think that what others have to offer is more valuable than our own gifts and talents. During these moments of self-doubt, remind yourself that you are valuable, you are an asset, and you have a voice. Remind yourself that you can make good, sound decisions, you will not be controlled by your feelings, and you can think critically and soundly to resolve any conflict. I have experienced plenty of days of self-doubt, but the one thing I knew for sure was that going backwards was not an option. Once you hold on to that truth, you, too, will continue to move forward in your new way of thinking, speaking, acting, and believing. You are the boss—the Break Up Boss—of your life!

Before this chapter ends, repeat this affirmation again. "*I believe in myself! I believe in myself! I believe in myself!*" I believe in you, too!

CHAPTER FIVE
REFLECTIONS

Are you ready for the ultimate breakup with yourself? Why or why not?

_____

_____

_____

_____

_____

_____

_____

_____

_____

_____

_____

_____

_____

_____

_____

In this chapter, we discussed your thoughts and the role they play in your decision-making and self-perception. What thoughts have you had about yourself in the past? What is your perception of yourself?

_____

_____

_____

_____

_____

_____

_____

_____

_____

_____

_____

_____

_____

_____

_____

_____

_____

_____

We learned that our emotions can fool us at times, and sometimes, they can cause us to make the wrong decisions. How have your feelings gotten you in trouble in the past? What will you do moving forward to safeguard your emotions?

_____

_____

_____

_____

_____

_____

_____

_____

_____

_____

_____

_____

_____

_____

_____

_____

_____

_____

_____

We discussed value and self-worth in detail. In what ways will you give yourself value and focus on increasing your self-worth?

_____

_____

_____

_____

_____

_____

_____

_____

_____

_____

_____

_____

_____

_____

_____

_____

_____

_____

—

Lastly, we discussed the power and importance of believing in yourself. What steps will you take to believe in yourself, especially when you may receive backlash from those around you?

_____

_____

Now That You're Out, Stay Out!

Poem: Freedom

"Freedom"

I'm free, I'm free, I'm free to be me!
No more pain and misery!
You held me down for far too long.
You shut down my voice, and now I'll sing my song!
I hated all the things that you kept me from.
I wanted them so much, and I beat my own drum.
But now is the time for me to be free!
I will fly, I will sing, I will dance, then I will
have my glee!
My spirit is free; my heart is unchained.
My mind has been loosed, and things will never
be the same!
I love myself far too much. I love myself, and nothing
but the best will do.
My freedom is from me, but most of all, my freedom
is being away from you!
—Jeanine Mack, 3/2/2017

6

Chapter 6: Now That You're Out, Stay Out!

Chapter 6: Now That You're Out, Stay Out!

You now have all the tools you need to break free from negative, unloving, and unproductive relationships. Now, it's time for us to move on to a bigger and better life filled with love, peace, and joy! The best way to enjoy our new lives is to get to know ourselves better and appreciate the loving individual that's inside of us. I've prepared some very interesting and fun activities to assist you in getting to know yourself better and to help you understand what type of person would be a great match for you in your future relationship. Are you ready? I am! Now, let's go!

Personality Is Everything

You may have heard of Dr. Carl Jung and Dr. Isabel Briggs Myers, but if not, you may have heard of their work in the area of personality discovery. You may have even taken the

Myers-Briggs personality test during the screening process for your job. As a result of their research, they have identified sixteen personality types that are signified by four letters, such as ESTJ and INFP. The four letters briefly describe the traits of that personality type. For instance, ESTJ stands for Extrovert, Sensing, Telling, and Judgmental, while INFP stands for Introverted, Intuitive, Feeling, and Perceiving. According to my test results, my personality type is ENFP, or Extrovert, Intuitive, Feeling, and Perceiving. If you have never taken this personality test before, this will be fun for you, especially when you see your results. You can visit HumanMetrics.com7 to take a simplified version of their personality test and get your results. It's not timed, and there are no wrong answers. Just answer truthfully to get the best results.

Now that you have taken the personality test and have gotten your results, do you feel like the results were spot on or were you surprised by them? I hope you learned something new about your personality or reinforced what you already knew about yourself. Either way, this is a great starting point for getting to know yourself better and better understanding those around you, particularly when it comes to choosing a romantic partner. Some personality types naturally gel with one another, while others take some conscious effort to be compatible. I also hope, in taking the personality test, you had an aha moment where you realized why your past relationships didn't work out. Personality conflicts may have been at the core of your relationships' problems. Our personalities dictate multiple areas of our lives we may not realize, such as our career, our thought processes, our eating and sleeping habits, where we live, who we choose as friends, our fashion sense, mate selection—everything! Never underestimate the power of your personality. Get well acquainted with it, embrace who you are, and make adjustments as you learn and grow.

I've looked back on my personal experiences and can now see that personality conflicts played a major role in the demise of my relationships. I always attracted my exact opposite, which was cute and fun in the beginning, but in the long run, those combinations proved to be a disaster. These mismatches in personality types also played a role in the way I communicated with my partners. For instance, my extroverted personality type always conflicted with introverts because I wanted to speak out and discuss matters of conflict, while the introvert preferred to sit in thoughtful silence. I have a natural tendency to live in my feelings and express them openly, especially if I'm passionate about something. Conversely, my introverted partners were more logical in their expressions and interests. If I could give an example of what my past relationships looked like, I would say it would be like Beyoncé dating Ben Carson. Yeah, total opposites in every way.

What Do You Like?

So, what do you like? Has anyone ever asked you that question, and after an awkward moment of silence, you finally clear your throat and say, Reading, only to be asked, So, what are you reading? Yeah, we've all been there a time or two, but now is the time to discover what you truly like. Oftentimes, when we are in a relationship, we lose ourselves and become immersed in the interests of our partner. This is dangerous because you run the risk of neglecting your interests, friends, and family, ultimately becoming a clone of your partner. You were born a unique individual, and you bring your own set of qualities to the world. The saying "Why die a copy when you can live as an original?" always brings me back to reality when I feel myself falling victim to social assimilation.

In a scene from one of my favorite movies, Coming to America, Prince Akeem met his bride for the first time on their wedding day, but he didn't want to marry her because he didn't know her personally. So he stopped the ceremony and took her into a private room to try to get to know her before they took their vows. In the room, he asked her what she liked, and the beautiful bride responded, "Whatever you like." To his dismay, he quickly realized his bride had no interests of her own because she had been trained to like whatever he liked, and that's not what he wanted in a wife. He wanted to marry someone who had interests that were different from his. Likewise, you need to know what you like, so you can bring those interests to the table in a relationship.

You may not know what you like if you've always assimilated to the likes and dislikes of your past partners. The only way to find out if you like something is to try it. Don't be afraid or embarrassed, just step out with boldness and try new things, like ordering from a restaurant you've never been to before. My new thing is eating cooked sushi. I made some new friends, and they all love sushi, so in the spirit of following my own advice, I had to try it, and now I like it. You may want to try Caribbean, Cuban, German, authentic Italian, Indian, or Cajun food. Whatever it is, get out there, and try it. The server can help you order from the menu, so no worries there; just have fun with it. If you want, you can sign up for an art class, join a community softball team, visit a new city for a weekend, go skydiving, or take an acting class. This is your opportunity to define or redefine yourself. The more you develop your interests, the more interesting you will become to others, and most of all, you'll be more fulfilled as a person. You won't have the unnecessary need for another human being to define who you are and what you like. Make a commitment to yourself to try something new a few times a month. Your future self will thank you!

Positively Positive

Positive energy is contagious. As you start your new life as a whole and happy person, you'll need to have the confidence in yourself to move forward. If you have negative thoughts about yourself, you'll have a negative perception of yourself. It's time for those negative thoughts to go. The following positive affirmations are an excellent tool to get you started. You can speak these affirmations out loud first thing in the morning, during your lunch break, and even at night before going to bed. The more you profess these affirmations in your life, the more likely they will become a reality. Don't be shy. This is your life and your future, and it starts today!

- I have value and worth. I am not a failure, and success is in my future.
- I am intelligent, and I can make good decisions for myself.
- I am not afraid. Fear no longer exists in my life.
- I am happy, joyful, and at peace.
- I am pain- and drama-free. I do not accept negativity in my life.
- I am beautiful. I am lovable. I am enough.
- God loves me unconditionally. I have nothing to prove to anyone.
- I am committed to being in good health. I will eat healthy, exercise consistently, and get regular health checkups.
- I will achieve my goals and dreams, no matter what happens.
- I am the CEO of my life; I will hire and fire accordingly.
- I have no need to compare myself to others because I am uniquely me.
- I will not accept less than what I deserve in life and in love.
- I love myself.

I love positive affirmations because when you hear these positive words come out of your mouth, you stand a little taller, feel a little stronger and happier, think clearer, and most of all, you start to believe in yourself again. You must learn to believe in yourself and master being a whole person before you can invite another person into your heart and space. Ultimately, we attract who we are, so if you truly want to be in a happy and fulfilled relationship, you need to become a happy and fulfilled individual. You don't need outside influences to validate you. Simply pull from your inner strength. Remember, you are the Boss!

CHAPTER SIX REFLECTIONS

After taking the personality quiz, which personality type are you? Do you think your personality type plays a role in who you choose as a mate?

_____

_____

_____

_____

_____

_____

_____

_____

_____

_____

Now that you're ready to discover your interests, what activities, restaurants, places, or things would you like to try?

_____

_____

_____

_____

_____

_____

_____

_____

_____

_____

_____

_____

Which positive affirmations in this chapter were difficult for you to say about yourself? Why do you think that is?

_____

_____

_____

_____

_____

_____

_____

_____
_____
_____
_____
_____
_____
_____

Do you feel like you're the boss of your life? What do you need to do to improve your self-confidence?

_____
_____
_____
_____
_____
_____
_____
_____
_____
_____
_____
_____
_____
_____
_____
_____
_____
_

Forgive and
Remember

Poem: "The Bridge"

"The Bridge"

I've been here before; it's like déjà vu.
I'm standing here alone, and then I see you.
We love, we wonder, we fight, we leave.
Now I'm standing here alone again,
but I can barely breathe.
This is the Bridge that I never cross for fear of loss,
The loss of you and me to be happy,
but we are not meant to be.
You see, I've got this thing where I keep
repeating my past.
It's you with me but in different places,
spaces, and different faces,
But still the same insecurities and issues
and hurts and pains.
I hate that I don't love me more than I love you;
it's insane!
I've got to cross this Bridge to get to my Light
and one true love.

This dangerous repetition is killing my ambition
for more from above.
I tried to forget my past, but I need to remember,
So that this time next September,
I would have crossed the Bridge.
—Jeanine Mack, September 2017

7

Chapter 7: Forgive and Remember

Chapter 7: Forgive and Remember

"If you do what you've always done, you'll get what you've always gotten." This thought-provoking quote from the esteemed Tony Robbins is so relevant in the area of relationships because, as creatures of habit, we have an innate tendency to repeat our past mistakes and relationship failures. It would make sense to not repeat the pain we've experienced, but time and time again, we end up single, battered, bruised, hurt, and confused, with no clue as to how we have arrived at that place yet again in our relationships. The answer to this reckless dilemma is revealed in Tony Robbins' quote. We keep doing what we've always done; and therefore, we keep yielding the same results.

Doing What You've Always Done

If you are like me, after each one of my relationship breakups, I found myself zoning out and asking myself, How did I manage to lose another romantic relationship? It has taken me many years to learn this hard lesson, so I hope you will learn from my pain and misfortune. I finally came to the conclusion that I kept the same mindset when choosing my next partner, and I also kept the same low self-esteem and negative perception of myself. Please understand, my friend; how you view or perceive yourself and the world around you will determine how you make your decisions. You simply cannot make better choices for yourself using the same brain you used to make the bad ones. The crazy thing is the people around you notice the crash-and-burn pattern you're in, but the only one who can put a stop to it is you.

Let's be honest with ourselves here; how many disagreements have you had with your close friends, family, and well-meaning co-workers about the new person you're so head over heels for? Then, after a few days, weeks, months, or years of temporary pleasure and numerous episodes of heartache, you come back to those same people with the realization that their initial warnings were accurate? Yes, he was moving too fast for you. Yes, she was out of your league. No, you were not financially ready to take on an instant family. Yes, you do come from two different worlds. No, you have nothing in common but your physical attraction. Yet, somehow, we still convince ourselves that "it can work," and everyone else is wrong about him or her. In actuality, we were the ones who were wrong. Wrong thinking led to poor decisions in choosing our mates.

Change Your Mind, Change Your Life

Here's the good news: You can change your mind. How? By doing exactly what you're doing right in this moment: reading a book that is educating you, encouraging you, empowering you, and equipping you with the essential tools to help you grow in your understanding and knowledge. You can also seek out successful couples who have been happily married for more than fifteen years. They can offer helpful tips on the ins and outs of what it takes to stay together. Attending relationship conferences is also helpful because they offer a plethora of information in the form of various speakers, books, and materials about how to be a better single person before trying to seek out a relationship. And, of course, taking some well-needed "me time" to reflect on and write down your wants and needs and what went wrong can help you get to the bottom of your unhealthy patterns. These are all excellent resources to help you change your mindset and lead you on the path to new and improved decision-making in your relationships and in your life.

Right now, admit the following to yourself: I need help with changing my mindset about relationships. I no longer want to be in this crash-and-burn cycle. This may be hard for some of you to admit to yourself, but I, too, have had to admit this to myself more than once, and I didn't enjoy swallowing that tough pill. My pride and ego were bruised, but more than that, my heart hurt. I realized that healing my heartache was more of a priority than feeding my pride and stroking my ego. I knew a better life was available to me because I saw it all around me; however, it was eluding me simply because my mindset would not allow me to grasp a new way of thinking. I'm so happy I have access to social media and friends who tag me in posts by relationship coaches, motivational speakers, ministers, authors, and artists who share life-changing tips, advice, books, speeches, art, and inspiration. So my question to you, my friend, is are you ready to change your mind?

It's Time to Forgive

Forgiving yourself and your ex-partners is a major component that can keep you from repeating your past relationship blunders. I think it's important to define what forgiveness is and what it is not. According to the Merriam-Webster Online Dictionary, "forgive" is defined as follows:

Transitive verb: 1a: to give up resentment of or claim to requital for, forgive an insult

b: to grant relief from payment of, forgive a debt

2: to cease to feel resentment against (an offender): pardon, forgive one's enemies

Intransitive verb: to grant forgiveness, had to learn to forgive and forget

I agree with this definition of forgive; however, the last

part of the intransitive verb definition suggests that you "forgive and forget," but allow me to recommend that you forgive and remember. Forgetting your past hurt and pain eventually becomes the blinder that keeps you from seeing the potential relationship trouble you came away from, and that same blindness can cause you to repeat the crash-and-burn cycle again with your new partner. I don't want you to dwell on your past pain nor allow it to put you in a negative emotional place. Instead, you should use it as a learning point and a warning sign, as we discussed in Chapter 2, to help you avoid repeating that pain. Forgiving yourself and your ex-partner will allow you to heal mentally, emotionally, and spiritually from the trauma you endured in that relationship. If you are like me, you are probably harder on yourself than anyone else, so give yourself a break, show yourself some love and understanding, and most of all, forgive yourself.

I can recall the tremendous burden I felt while signing my divorce papers for the second time. I felt lost, stupid, dejected, disappointed, and ashamed. Hadn't I learned my lessons from the problems and failure of my first marriage? Why was this happening to me again almost ten years later? But here's the reality of my situation: I still hadn't forgiven myself for the failure of my first marriage (not that I am admitting to being the cause of the breakup because, of course, it takes two to make or break a relationship). I just never really took the time to heal from the issues surrounding it. I can now admit that I never forgave my ex-husband because, every day, I was reminded of the divorce, whether that reminder came in the form of a lack of finances to take care of our three sons, the emotional health of our children, or my living arrangement. All of these issues and more leaked themselves into my second marriage, and ultimately, the end result was the same. That realization was not only my experience but that of my ex-spouse, as well. He also had his own set of unresolved issues that went unchecked in his marriages. Unresolved personal conflicts can really take a toll on a relationship. It is our individual responsibility to recognize these areas of deficiency within ourselves and those we choose to be in a relationship with. Ignoring these areas or wishing them away will only lead to frustration and heartache later on.

Release the Burden

I cannot emphasize the importance of forgiving yourself and those who have wronged you enough. Yes, you read that correctly. You must forgive those who have wronged you. Your choice to forgive them doesn't mean they were right in their negative actions and words against you, nor does it justify their thinking and behavior. Forgiveness is not for the offender; it is for you. You need to be free of the hurt, pain, confusion, anger, bitterness, and negativity that person brought into your life. If you truly want to be free, happy, and whole again, you must forgive and remember. Don't allow your past to rob you of another day of your present and future happiness. You don't have to carry the burden of guilt and shame for losing a relationship you thought would last forever. Forgive yourself for choosing that person, ignoring the red flags, and allowing yourself to be treated harshly. You cannot control the actions and words of others, but you can certainly control yourself.

Remembering Your Milestones

One major benefit of remembering your past is your ability to measure your milestones and see your progress. For instance, when I was on one of my many "diets," I recorded my beginning weight then weighed myself weekly to track my progress toward my goal. I couldn't see my progress by just looking at my body in the mirror, so I would look back in my journal at my starting weight and the few pounds I had lost each week. Those two to three pounds a week eventually added up to ten pounds, then eighteen pounds, then twenty-five pounds, and finally, forty-seven pounds. Anytime I wanted to give up, had a setback, or got frustrated, I looked back on my past progress to see how far I had come. This motivated me to keep going and begin again.

Likewise, in the area of our relationships, we should set realistic goals for ourselves to accomplish over time. Please don't make the mistake of keeping these goals locked inside of your head. You must write them down, so you can hold yourself accountable and stay on track with the deadlines you've set. You can use the notes app on your cellphone or tablet, a Word document on your laptop, or just good, old-fashioned pen and paper to journal your progress. I bought five-subject notebooks because I like to draw in one section, write poetry, books, or my thoughts in another, and keep track of my hopes and dreams in another. As a matter of fact, this book was originally penned in my notebook. If I didn't have it, I would've lost the ideas and the material for this book. Writing is powerful; our minds can only retain so much information, and then it's gone. So do yourself a huge favor by designating a place where you can record your progress.

Have you ever heard the quotes, "You have to crawl before you walk," "Baby steps," or "Life is a marathon, not a sprint?" I used to hate these quotes because I like instant results. Patience is definitely something I'm working on; however, I have now come to understand that I cannot rush my process, and neither can you, my friend. We all have lessons to learn during our healing process. If we don't learn those lessons, we will ultimately repeat the hurt cycle and have to start from the beginning. Who has that kind of time? Not me and certainly not you! So don't try to rush your process; enjoy it, learn during it, heal, restore, reassess yourself, and come out better, stronger, and wiser on the other side. You can do it! I have done it, and I continue to do it in several areas of my life.

Change Your Thinking, Change Your Life

Change your thinking, and you'll change your perspective about yourself, your relationships, and your life. Change is not always easy, but it's always worth the effort because of the wonderful benefits you will gain over time. Remembering your past is an integral part of your forgiveness and healing process. Remembering what you've gone through will help you to not repeat those negative experiences and better recognize the warning signs when they appear in future relationships. Don't forget to forgive and love yourself. Never settle for less than the love, respect, and appreciation you deserve. There is no room for guilt, shame, and blame in your future happy life.

CHAPTER SEVEN
REFLECTIONS

How do you define forgiveness?

_____

_____

_____

_____

_____

_____

_____

_____

Have you forgiven yourself or others? If not, list who you need to forgive and how they hurt you, starting with yourself.

_____

_____

_____

_____

_____

_____

_____

_____

_____

_____

_____

_____

_____

_____

_____

_____

_____

_____

_____

_____

_____

_____

What can you do today to help safeguard yourself from becoming bitter about your past negative relationships?

_____

_____

_____

_____

_____

_____

_____

_____

_____

_____

_____

_____

_____

_____

_____

Final Thoughts and Conclusions

8

Chapter 8: Final Thoughts and Conclusions

Chapter 8: Final Thoughts and Conclusions

I have enjoyed taking this journey with you toward breaking free from bad relationships and self-defeat. I hope you've been able to discover your confidence in finding love in the future. Change is not always easy, but you made it through, and with each day, you will become the person you've always dreamed you could be, without having to fight with negative people and negative thoughts. Your goal is to always love and appreciate yourself, then those around you will follow suit.

As we discovered in Chapter 1, you must understand the reasons why you have gotten into the relationships you've endured in the past. Those main reasons included the Eye Candy Appeal, Lonely Hearts Club, Approval Ratings, Judgement Day, Religious Rights, and Financial Fantasy. All of these are the wrong reasons to get and stay in a relationship. We cannot begin to move forward until we can clearly understand the past. Always be sure of the reasons why you are seeking or entering a new romantic relationship.

Knowing when it's time to exit a bad relationship is paramount. In Chapter 2, we focused on recognizing the signs of when a relationship is over. Ignoring those signs in the past have proven to be detrimental to your happiness, and can ultimately guide you off course in every area of your life. Let's always take heed of those yellow caution flags and red warning flags. They are there for a reason, and that reason is to keep your heart and mind safe from being hurt.

Chapter 3 dealt with the issue of abuse and domestic violence in relationships. It's never OK to be abused in any form. Abuse is not love! You are worthy and deserving of love, respect, patience, and peace of mind. You are a special part of God's creation, and you have a special place in this world. Please make up your mind today to get out and get help if you are living in fear or are being hurt physically, mentally, or emotionally in any way. Please use the valuable resources I have placed at the end of this book or any resource that is readily available to you. A new and better life is waiting for you.

Chapter 4 gave us some examples of bad relationships and some strategies on how to effectively end them. Even though I may not have highlighted your exact relationship situation, you now have a starting point on how to safely and effectively end a relationship. The point here is to take control of your life and heart and feel comfortable enough to separate yourself when you are involved in a toxic relationship. There's no perfect time to break up with someone; however, you will cheat yourself out of future happy moments every day you remain in an expired relationship.

The Ultimate Breakup was surprisingly with yourself in Chapter 5. Although it's absolutely necessary to end those negative relationships, it's also equally important to end those bad habits within ourselves, such as negative thinking, emotional rollercoasters, low self-worth, and a lack of belief in ourselves. Some people around us may not celebrate our new sense of self-worth and self-confidence, and that's OK. All that matters is that we stay focused on reaching our goal of self-improvement.

Chapter 6 was our breakthrough chapter. Now you've broken free and are ready to start fresh as the boss of your new life. Discovering who you are and what you like is key in healing, staying on the path to falling back in love with yourself, and reclaiming your identity before pursuing love from others. This is an exciting time to be the version of yourself you've always wanted to be and experience new adventures, places, and things that were not possible for you while you were in a toxic relationship. Celebrate the new you! Smile, laugh, and enjoy being genuinely happy for yourself. Trust me, positive energy is contagious, and those around you will feel your newfound joy, too.

Chapter 7 afforded us with the opportunity to forgive and remember our past and use those hurtful experiences as stepping stones to enter a better future. Remembering the past is different from dwelling in it and feeling guilt or shame, but that's where forgiveness comes into play. You must forgive yourself and forgive those who have hurt you. Please keep in mind that forgiveness is not for them; it's for you! You cannot grow unless you forgive, heal, and love yourself. Harboring bitterness and bringing it into your next relationship will only lead you to another relationship failure. Don't allow your past to hinder you; allow it to help you become the awesome person you've always known you could be. In this chapter, we also learned the importance of measuring our progress and staying patient. Keep in mind the process of healing serves a purpose, and that purpose is for you to learn valuable lessons, so you don't repeat your past.

In conclusion, never forget that you are truly the CEO of your life, so hire and fire accordingly! You were born for greatness in every area of your life. No more settling for mediocrity. It's time to promote yourself to the boss of your life. You can do it, my friend! Just know that the Break Up Boss has your back. Go now and conquer in peace, love, and Bossiness!

Valuable Resources

- The National Domestic Abuse Hotline

  Call 1-800-799-SAFE (7233)
  or visit online at TheHotline.org

- Jane Doe, Inc.—The Massachusetts Coalition Against Sexual Assault and Domestic Violence

  Call 1-877-785-2020 or visit online at JaneDoe.org

- National Coalition Against Domestic Violence (NCADV)

  Call 303-839-1852, Email mainoffice@ncadv.org, or visit online at NCADV.org

- Healthy Place, America's Mental Health Channel

Visit online at HealthyPlace.com

- Center for Relationship Abuse Awareness

  Visit online at StopRelationshipAbuse.org

- Florida Coalition Against Domestic Violence (FCADV)
  Call the Florida Domestic Violence Hotline at 1-800-500-1119 or visit online at FCADV.org/ florida-domestic-violence-hotline-1-800-500-1119

Positive Affirmations for Your Heart, Mind and Soul

These positive affirmations are based on the content of this book and the various seasons of my life. You can write these on sticky notes and place them on your bathroom mirror or your computer at work to remind yourself to speak positive things into your life. Recite them loud and proud or even whisper them. Whatever you do, just speak it, and watch how much your life changes for the better!

- I love myself!
- I have value and worth. I am not a failure, and success is in my future.
- I am intelligent, and I can make good decisions for myself.
- I am not afraid. Fear no longer exists in my life.
- I am happy, joyful, and at peace.
- I am pain- and drama-free. I do not accept negativity in my life.
- I am beautiful. I am lovable. I am enough.
- God loves me unconditionally. I have nothing to

prove to anyone.
- I am committed to being in good health. I will eat healthy, exercise consistently, and get regular health checkups.
- I will achieve my goals and dreams, no matter what happens.
- I am the CEO of my life; I will hire and fire accordingly.
- I have no need to compare myself to others because I am uniquely me.
- I will not accept less than what I deserve in life and in love.
- I am strong. Weakness no longer rules my thoughts.
- I will shine my light of love, peace, and joy everywhere I go.
- My smile makes me happy, and it lights up any room.
- I will manage my finances and credit to work for me, not against me.
- Money is a tool I use to buy what I need. I am not controlled by money.
- I will be better today than I was yesterday.
- I speak life and Light into my life.
- I believe in myself.

- I will fulfill the purpose and destiny of my life. No more wasting time on meaningless people or activities.

Poetic Reflections

Soulmate

Soulmate? I can't relate!
You mean, my date or my late ex or that one I loved but
turned out to be a hex?
Soulmate? A perfect match for my soul?
You mean, my wounded heart where love departed a long
time ago? Or the place where love grew and abode?
Oh, wait! You mean, my one true love,
The one who can get me in my feelings and then gimme
that "sexual healing."
Oh, the one who keeps me on the phone until 3 a.m.,
talkin' 'bout our past, present, and future fam.
It's the one who makes me feel like we've known each
other for "a couple of forevers."
A soulmate seems like an urban myth more than a gift.
But one thing is for sure: My soulmate is now secure.
My lover, my friend, my ride or die til' the end.
Never has love tasted so sweet, been such a treat, been so
unique.
Soulmate? Yeah…I can relate.

—Jeanine Mack, April 2016

Missing You

M - Maybe you are missing me, too.
I - Imagine what I am going through.
S - Sad and worried about you.
S – Soon, call me because I'm blue.
I – If you truly love me, you must cleave.
N – Never leave. Please, Baby, please.
G – Going to love you through infinity!
You, you, you, oh, you!
Just you, just you, just you.
I'm really missing you, really missing you.

—Jeanine Mack, November 2003

I Know When a Man....

I know when a man loves me.

He holds me, he touches me, he smells me,

He reaches for me in the night, he sacrifices for me.

He works for me, he lives for me, he likes me.

He looks into my eyes to view my soul, he encourages me, he lusts after me,

He thinks about me, he takes care of my needs, he makes love to me.

He is willing to die for me…

but

I know when a man doesn't love me.

He ignores me, he resents me, he no longer shares my space.

He breaks my spirit, he blows out my flames, he hates me,

He won't have sex with me, he avoids me, he doesn't call me.

He won't come home to me, he doesn't need me, he hates me.

He is willing to live without me…

so

This is how I know a man…

—Jeanine Mack, August 2009

Secret Admirer

I hate that I love you so much!
You made me cry when I had no tears, only fears.
How can I have so much love for someone who doesn't know I exist?
I scream, "I love you!" My mouth is wide open, but no sound comes out;
What the hell is this about?
My chest hurts with heaviness because my love is unexpressed.
I have visions of our bodies tangled with hot sweat. I pant heavily in your face,
Your arrogant arms squeeze me in passion; what an embrace!
I dream of soft, tender kisses in the golden, honey sunset,
Your mouth pressed against mine, so sticky, so wet.
Your thick tongue whips inside my mouth like an untamed bull.
You push, you buck, I suck, I pull.
I've got to get my mind off of you; you don't even know me!
You have your unruly life, so brazen, so free.
All I need is one lucky fateful chance to let you feel my

pulse; I am alive!

I live, I breathe, I bleed, I long for you to come to me.

I want your freedom but not to enslave you with my hate or jealousy.

Just touch me with your freedom, and my love will rest in peace.

I hate yo' ass!

—Jeanine Mack, August 2009

Cardiac Arrest

It's nothing like having your heart stolen by the Love Thief, or did you willingly give it because you were in grief?

The Love Thief is slick and smooth, so fluid, so careful to put you in the mood.

Slowly, but surely, you feel the injection of disappointment, disrespect, and rejection.

Now you're flatlining on the monitor. No aid in sight. Somebody call the Love Doctor!

Clear! And the compressions start. Reviving your heart is gonna be so hard!

All the years of brokenness, baggage, and hopefulness, yet raggedness.

Still no response, flatlined on the screen. The Love Doctor is losing you; do you know what that means?

It's time to catch the Love Thief to retrieve your cure. Now you're on Love Support to help you endure.

The Thief don't wanna give it up, but now he's surrounded. Twenty counts of cardiac arrest, no more rebounding!

Beat, beat, beat. Your heart is up and running! Let's thank the Love Doctor and avoid the Thief, so cunning.

Protect your heart at all costs. Show the Love Thief who's the boss!

No more cardiac arrest for you. Keep the Love Doctor on speed dial, and she'll be there for you.

—Jeanine Mack, August 2010

He Say He A Man

He say he a man 'cause he works hard chasing paper without the deadly caper.

He say he a man 'cause he does all he can to make me glad. He's the best I ever had!

He say he a man 'cause when I cry on his shoulder, he's as strong as a boulder.

He say he a man 'cause he steps into his shoes, no straps, no lacing, just hard bottoms, and he's smooth!

He say he a man 'cause pressure doesn't break him, shake him, stress him, just makes him more of a man.

He say he a man 'cause he knows how to arouse my body with his soft kisses, caresses, and granting my fantasies and wishes.

He say he a man 'cause he's got vision and focus. His dreams won't be stolen by haters or eaten by locusts.

He say he a man 'cause no other man can take his place, occupy his space, or walk in his grace.

He say he a man 'cause I say he is a man, and he's my man. We're walking hand in hand, taking our shining light to this dark land.

He is a man!
—Jeanine Mack, 12/1/2011

2 For 1

I really love him. He's my ideal man.
I lust to share his breath whenever I can.
His essence, his scent is so intoxicating!
My body jerks in passion pains while masturbating.
I must have him! I must touch him softly, slowly...
His sweaty skin, I lick, lick, lick...
The time goes by, tick, tick, tick...
Our bodies behave like naughty school children
Playing behind the oak tree, discoverin'
Something sinful, yet heavenly. He raptures me...
He lets me be me. I have no regret for loving him!
No, I cannot lie. This man possess me at my will.
He's breathing life into me that I can feel.
I'm filled with a jealous rage when he leaves me alone.
I want to take him home.
Sadly, hatefully, shamefully, I cannot take him
home with me
Because there is another man at home, you see?
My rock, my keeper, my sanity,
He helps me, he listens to me, he selflessly cares for me.
So how can I love another so carelessly?
Don't judge or rebuke me; put down your stones!

'Cause I've never spoken in evil tones.
Sometimes a "good man" just ain't good enough.
Not enough passion, heat, life, mystery…
Just not enough for me!
He's too perfect, too high, too Ivy League.
I need all that, but something's still missin'.
It's my ideal man, so that's why I'm dippin'!
I've been thrust into this love race, so I'll run.
My life is worth living when there's 2 for 1.

—Jeanine Mack, August 2009

Revenge

Revenge, Revenge, you're my friend.
Through the good and the bad, you've helped me win!
I need you like a dope head needs a drug.
One thing is for sure: You've replaced Love.
Oh, Revenge, your taste is so sweet.
You fill me up with joy, and my heart skips a beat.
I lust for your schemes to punish my enemies.
I can't wait to see them crushed and worried.
Revenge, you lead me down some pretty dark paths,
But my enemies deserve my anger, my wrath!
People should beware before crossing me.
Revenge and I will ensure they don't sleep.
I'm the Queen of Karma; I'll be sure you get yours.
No worries, fools, you'll get more and more.
Revenge, Revenge, you are my only friend.
And because of you, I always win!

—Jeanine Mack, December 2017

The Greatest Mystery

Knock, knock. Who's at the door? I open it, but no one is there…hmmm.

Ring, ring. It's the telephone. The caller ID reads "Unknown." I answer it, but no one is there, only silence.

Honk, honk! A car horn blows outside. I look through the window, but no one is there. Interesting.

Thud, thud! My heart is pounding inside my chest!

I'm afraid because I am alone.

Suddenly, air fills my nostrils, and I awaken to your lovely face, your warm embrace, the breath of life you breathe into me.

For, you see, it was just a dream about the greatest mystery

Of how someone like you could love someone like me so unconditionally.

Just afraid you will awake and see me for who I really be. Maybe your blinded love does see me, and that…that…that is the greatest mystery.

—Jeanine Mack, 10/7/2003

Sweet Ambition

Sweet Ambition, do I need permission to express myself to you? There are some people who cross your path, even if they aren't meant to last. It makes you forget your past, to grasp the chance to let your love shine through.

Sweet Ambition, my love is in remission ever since the day I met you. It's that thing you do with your lips when you smile. The depth of your voice makes me want to talk awhile. I'm inhaling your presence to the point of intoxication. Have I made myself clear? I don't want to be in fear.

Sweet Ambition, did I fail to mention there's something really special about you? Your unwavering peace and quiet strength make me feel secure. For you, any storm I would endure. I long to be in your embrace, and maybe one day, your lips will bless my face.

Sweet Ambition, you've started a revolution of my love evolution for you! You have become my friend, my confidant, my lover, my family, my real protectant. My rock, my shield, I stop, and you yield…to my needs, so that I can feel your love for me.

Sweet Ambition, I thank you for completing your mission of bringing sweet love to me!

—Jeanine Mack, 12/14/17

References

(Listed in the order they appeared within the text)

1. "For the Love of Money." Retrieved October 6, 2018 from YouTube http://youtu.be/GXE_n2q08Yw
2. Abuse. (n.d.). Retrieved February 22, 2017 from https://www.merriam-webster.com/dictionary/abuse
3. Love. (n.d.). Dictionary.com Unabridged. Retrieved February 23, 2017 from Dictionary.com website http://www.dictionary.com/browse/love
4. National Statistics. National Coalition Against Domestic Violence. Retrieved March 1, 2017 from http://ncadv.org/learn-more/statistics
5. Whitener, Svetlana. (2018). "How Your Emotions Influence Your Decisions". Retrieved September 6, 2018 from http://www-forbes-com.cdn.ampproject.org
6. Value. (n.d). Retrieved November 7, 2018 from https://www.dictionary.com/browse/value
7. Jung Typology Test. (1998-2017). Retrieved May 23, 2017 from http://www.humanmetrics.com/personality
8. Forgive. (n.d). Retrieved October 1, 2017 from

https://www.merriam-webster.com/dictionary/for-give

9. Jensen–Salisbury, Karen (n.d.). "What to do when life doesn't make sense: Think About What You're Thinking About." Retrieved October 6, 2018 from the Bible App devotional plan.

About the Author

Jeanine Mack grew up in the Greater Daytona Beach area as the youngest of six children. She is a 1992 graduate of Mainland High School. At the tender age of nineteen years old, she married her first husband and was blessed with three sons from that union—Christian, Xavier, and Kingsley—whom she boasts are the jewels in her crown. Sadly, that union ended in divorce, and many years later, she remarried and eventually found herself single once again. It was through the experiences of these two broken marriages, divorces, and several dating relationships that Jeanine began to focus on her pursuit of healing, personal empowerment, self-discovery, and knowledge about relationship dynamics.

A few of Jeanine's academic accomplishments include the completion of her associate of arts degree at Daytona State College and later graduating from Warner University with a bachelor of arts in organizational management. While tackling the tall task of single-motherhood and working full time, Jeanine attended the prestigious Embry-Riddle Aeronautical University, where she earned her master of science in leadership. Accomplishing this seemingly daunting feat gave Jeanine the ability to realize her own strength and capabilities for achieving her dreams.

The coupling of Jeanine's strong academic background and professional work experiences allowed her to hone in on her leadership and listening skills and her ability to be empathetic to the needs of those around her. With the skills inside her professional toolbox and her caring, maternal heart, Jeanine felt the calling to help hurting people overcome their pasts and empower them to catapult themselves into a bright, happy, and whole future. Although the fulfillment of her calling has not been easy or instantaneous, Jeanine is committed, ready, and able to heal heavy hearts, one person at a time.

At the publishing of this book, Jeanine has remained happy, confident, and peaceful in her personal space and in her singleness. Her healing journey is a work in progress, and she hopes to continue to inspire others to begin and commit to their healing journey by sharing her process with them.

Author Resources

More Books from Author Jeanine Elise Mack are available now on Amazon.com and at www.Mack-MediaMoguls.com

Life Lessons Series for children ages 3yrs-9yrs:

1. What Is He? **(Available in Spanish!)**
2. Grammy and Me **(Available in Spanish!)**
3. You're Not My Daddy! **(Available in Spanish!)**
4. Momma's New Baby **(Available in Spanish!)**
5. Big Bad Billy **(Available in Spanish!)**

Jeanine is available for speaking and book reading engagements.
Please contact her through Mack Media Moguls, LLC via email, phone or regular mail as follows:

Mack Media Moguls, LLC

P.O. Box 781318

Orlando, FL 32878

MackMediaMogulsLLC@gmail.com **/Daily**

407-900-7435/ Monday – Friday, 9am-7pm EST

www.MackMediaMoguls.com /Daily

Subscribe for updates and special offers!